When Did Bad Language Become So Good?

---

7 Formulas for overcoming bad language

BARIBELA IDRIS

When Did Bad Language Become So Good?
Copyright © 2020 Baribela Idris. All rights reserved.

Requests for information should be addressed to:
bela@baribelaidris.com

This book, or parts thereof, may not be reproduced, stored in a retrieval system, or transmitted in any form or by any means, electronic, mechanical, photocopying, recording or otherwise, without the written permission of the publisher.

Published By: Baribela Idris

978-0-6487534-5-2 (Paperback)
978-0-6487534-6-9 (eBook)

Printed in Australia

Dedication

To all those who believe that words have the power to create, heal and transform lives for the best. Also, for those who need encouragement to make speaking a good language a habit.

Thank you for being here

By reading this book and providing a review, you are adding more value to its content and spreading a much-needed positive message for the future generation.

Thank you for recycling the message in this book

Best regards
Baribela Idris

CONTENTS

Introduction 1

Chapter 1: What Is So Good About Bad Language? 5

Chapter 2: You've Got The Power 22

Chapter 3: A Cancer Of Emotional Expression 38

Chapter 4: What About The Next Generation? 51

Chapter 5: The Rise Of Cussing –
The Global Warming Effect 66

Chapter 6: When You Can't Help Yourself 75

Chapter 7: The Beautiful Truth 87

Introduction

Words have a life of their own. Once spoken, they have the power to hurt, please, and change destinies because they are heard by the heart. Their final target is the heart. Our words have a powerful influence on our family, business, spirituality, career, community, and marriage.

"What the beep?!", "Shut the beep up!", "You beep!", You're full of beep!". Expressions like these are what you sometimes hear on the 6pm news as the journalists seek to "beep" out the swear words. An attempt to fine-tune and keep the story real as it comes across the airwaves to audiences. Newscasters that want to tell a story as it really happened, but still wish to protect the delicate ears of the children listening. A reporter that wants to manage the frequency and pollution caused by swearing.

My focus in this book is addressing the direct and current effects cussing/cursing or swearing has on a daily and long-term basis, and the value of the language that we control. I will explore the effects of the "F" "S" "B" and other negative, crass, and profane words as spoken regularly by good citizens. I will be discussing the importance of having standards that will help you control or cut swearing. I dare to share these truths about how we can control or eliminate the obsession with cussing.

Cursing is like going on a quest to gather dirt into the house. Why would anyone want to do that? It makes your house messy and gives you the extra task of cleaning, which you don't need.

This world is everyone's space and as humans, one of our greatest needs is each other - "No man is an island." We share this space, whether we speak positively or negatively as we journey through life. Your everyday words have an enormous impact on how the day plays out, either with your mood or your tasks.

Words are as alive as the hundreds of bacteria in our mouths. What you and I say will affect the people we love and the people we don't agree with. That is why it is important to think and consider what we are about to say before we utter words out of our mouths.

Our words can trigger intense emotions and reactions that can strengthen or estrange us from one another. The funny thing is, we need each other. We need each other, to buy and sell, challenge, love, procreate, protect, communicate, have jobs, or go on holidays. We exist for each other as strange as that may sound. Therefore, it is essential and for our benefit that we try and do the best we can for each other, and it starts with what we can control; our words, and how we use them.

If you belong to a group where there are no standards in the way you speak, then it is not a healthy environment. Perhaps, you are ignoring the standards. Then I hope that at the end of this book, you will reconsider your stance.

"So then, my beloved brethren, let every man be swift to hear, slow to speak, slow to wrath; for the wrath of man does not produce the righteousness of God." - **James 1:19-20**

Simply put, be a good listener, watch and be careful with what you say, and don't get upset too easily because God expects a better standard from us. It also shows there is a connection between what we hear, how we speak and how we choose to react.

"Kind words can be short and easy to speak, but their echoes are truly endless." **— Mother Teresa**

Telling a child not to play with fire doesn't mean you don't love them. It means don't play with fire otherwise you will get burnt. This is about communicating the truth with love intended.

Don't play with fire.

The solution to making cussing an exception and not the norm or getting rid of it is not just the steps you take. It requires your understanding of the formulas before the steps so that there can be consistency. Without the formula, there is no solution. I will show you the formula needed to overcome this challenge.

Problems target the heart, so I will be showing you 7 formulas to the solutions that also target the heart. When the heart understands a matter, the resolution can begin. Any step-by-step instruction you receive becomes easier to follow because your heart is ready. I hope you will receive a positive transformation through the 7 formulas in this book.

CHAPTER 1

WHAT IS SO GOOD ABOUT BAD LANGUAGE?

Words have no power to impress the mind without the exquisite horror of their reality."

– Edgar Allan Poe

Honesty or Venting?

I was in a round-about and had a right of way when the car on my left almost entered the round-about at the same time. From her car, I could read her lips as she said, "f*** me" (yes, I can lipread those words). She was addressing herself as a response to her action. I had to veer somewhat to stop myself from hitting her car. I said to myself, "Thank God, that was close."

"If You Swear a Lot, You Are More Honest – Science Says So," was the title of an article I read recently. It got me thinking. Are we confusing the expression of frustration, anger, sadness, insults, and surprise with honesty and boldness?

All Fun and Games Until...

Playing with words is very satisfying, especially when those words are getting the reaction you want from your target audience. 'F'ing and 'S' ing may feel good when it makes the next person laugh and everyone seems to blend in with the moment. No tensions or objections. Good people, just having a chat and living a normal life, and there is absolutely nothing wrong with that.

That is exactly what the flesh wants. It's all fun and games until someone gets angry or there is a disagreement, then the intensity, tone, reaction, and frequency, of the 'F' ing and 'S' ing suddenly changes the atmosphere. No matter how good and smart you are, your flesh will easily yield to react back to what have been said unless you have trained your heart not to do so. Words that come out of the mouth in those delicate moments, can hurt many people for a long time and in fact cast a shadow on your integrity. Training your heart to respond with appropriate words may be the miracle you need, to speak a good language that will save you in that moment.

Here are some justifications I've come across as reasons to why cussing sounds appealing. Some may agree, and others may not:

- It's a preferred way to release anger.
- It's okay to cuss yourself when you accidentally break a plate or stub your toe. It doesn't affect anyone else.
- It's no big deal, it's just another word.
- Everyone else is doing it.
- It's part of the culture, don't take that from me.
- Where is the fun in life, if I can't belt out a few crass words now and again?
- I am not religious so that is not my cup of tea.
- I can say whatever I want.
- Research says people who swear are more honest, so I'm good.

I guess those are interesting reasons, but I beg to differ. My views are be mindful of words that soothe negative emotions for a moment but perpetuate the root of those vehement words for a protracted time. Pursue a lifestyle around long-term positive and fulfilling results.

When foul language is so bad that it feels good, watch out for the direction, and influence it's going to have on yourself and those around you.

What is Swearing?

Search the word "swearing" on Google and some definitions and examples it offers are:

Swearing

- the use of offensive language.
  "there's a lot of swearing in the show".

Swear

- make a solemn statement or promise undertaking to do something or affirming that something is the case.

Similar words include promise, vow, promise under oath, pledge one's self, take an oath, swear on the Bible, give an undertaking.

> *"He forced them to swear an oath of loyalty to him."*
> *"I've been sworn to secrecy".*

- use offensive language, especially as an expression of anger.

Similar words include curse, cuss, blaspheme, utter profanities, be foul-mouthed, bad language, foul language, take the Lord's name in vain, damn, obscenity.

"Peter swore under his breath".

I had to ask myself, *"When did bad language become so good?"*

One of my thoughts is that "Swearing can take the grammatical sense out of a sentence".

What Are You Really Saying?

Check out the Collins Dictionary meaning of some cuss words that are used daily, just to mention a few:

- *Shit: faeces; an act of defecation*
- *Fuck: an act of sexual intercourse*
- *Dick: slang word for a man's penis*
- *Ass/Arse: buttocks*
- *Cunt: offensive word for a female vagina*

- *Pussy: an informal name for a cat; a rude reference of the vagina*
- *Bitch: female dog*
- *Whore: a prostitute*

Basically, they are words and slangs that describe the animal and human body wastes or excretion, sexual acts, and animal and human body parts.

Now think of these words and more being said:

- After every other word
- In unique combinations like ordering food in a restaurant
- To explain every frustration
- In specific places
- Day in day out
- To express different emotions
- To explain situations
- When providing an instruction

I think after a while, it becomes:

- Mentally exhausting
- Frustrating

- Cheap talk
- Aggressive and violent in sound
- No longer funny

After having a visual of the meaning of these swear expressions, is it thus necessary to use swear words to describe the circumstance? Remember that words are alive. You and I were created into existence with spoken words and we can create and make changes with our spoken words every day.

You might say the actual interpretation is not what is implied, but they are not the right words either. In context, swear words are emotionally driven and abrasive in their use.

Submerged in Filth

There are homes, marriages, relationships, offices, communities, and even nations submerged with the mess created through these words. Words are alive. You may not see it now, but it will reflect in your spiritual, physical, social, and psychological state of wellbeing.

The disproportionate use of phrases, like cussing, intending insult leaves a terrible effect on the mental state of any human being. The clean-up process is more complex.

The Odd Ball

It's almost a shameful thing in some surroundings to be the only person not cursing at every turn. I applaud anyone that can stand their ground and uphold their morals, because peer pressure is a true pressure. Specifically, for someone trying to break out of that habit, it can be a challenge when among peers. It's like having a fridge full of alcohol when you are trying to stop a drinking habit. Each time you open the fridge, it's inviting and becomes even more problematic.

Sometimes, individuals have grown up in a surrounding where they are barraged with lazy words often, and it develops into second nature for them to speak in the same manner. It may look simpler to just go with the flow. In other scenario's, you may be in the presence of a clergy or in a conversation, and an apology will suffice, not because it is acceptable but because everyone is doing it, and no one wants to be judgemental.

Is it any better on the society when we type swear words to describe what we are saying with pretty stars in between, like Sh*t, F**k? Perhaps it is easier to accept and use, but the irony is mind-boggling.

Language in the Battle of Equality

A survey carried out in the United Kingdom in 2016 indicated that while men have drastically reduced their use of the F*** word, women, on the other hand, have significantly increased. The survey concluded that with the word "equality" in every sector of society, it is preposterous that female's expression of vulgar language should be any different from men. It is now a thing of the past to imagine qualifying any action as a gentlemanly behaviour or a ladylike language.

This survey is evidence of where language has been wrapped in the battle for equality, and this is not a new thing. There is a part of us as humans that may respond to that battle in a manner that wants to prove our equality to the world. I believe that unless we focus on speaking and living right by dealing with issues of the heart in a way that pleases God, we will never truly understand where to draw the line for both ladies and gentlemen.

The Snake in the Grass

Swearing in the matter of equality is like the snake in the green grass. The lines of what should be said, and how it should be said when building a relationship is so critical. If your focus is more about speaking at the same crass level as the next man or woman, then there is trouble. It's like been struck by a green snake in a green grass. You may not see it coming. The damage from your spoken words would have already released its poison before you know it.

It is interesting to know that the sense of equality or inequality, is still one of the greater conflicts and causes of relationships or marriages breaking down in society today.

Referred to the Boss

Standards are important in life. As a profession have jargons that make sense and bring clarity within that profession, so standards in our grammar bring clarity when used correctly. If you are working in an organisation, you are required to be up to standard with your job description. If you cannot meet the standards because you are a newbie or for whatever reason, you will be having a conversation with the boss.

I struggled with meeting up to my company's standard when I initially started work, because besides learning the skills required for the job, I had to put more effort into learning about new systems within the organisation that was completely different from what I was used to. It was a stressful time and I was almost sacked from my job.

However, I was fortunate with the help of my managers and mentors that were patient with me. As I was conscious of my accent at that time, I got nervous each time the phone rang, which distracted me from learning the job. That is another story.

My point is, there are standards and there are standards. Standards that make things work better, and standards that do the opposite. There are words we speak that will make our life better and others will do the opposite. Cussing and using profanity is one of such things. So, we need to have the right standards to enjoy life to the fullest.

The Influencer

The words I choose to utter are based on standards that can influence my life in positive ways to promote togetherness, selflessness, and better relationships with joy and longevity. It is a standard that works today and is based on the Word of God. In this case, God is the Boss and His word is the standard that works. I may get it wrong sometimes, but I know the path and just like any journey, I try and get back on track when I have missed it.

I have personally found that a lot of counselling techniques in solving issues are relatable to biblical principles. It's just like having a mentor that is experienced and has succeeded in the path you are about to take. It makes life easier; you go to them and have a good chat.

You do not have to be religious to want to reduce or eliminate the urge to swear at yourself or at others when life happens. Don't enjoy bad words. Let your conversations and interactions come under a civilized bracket for your benefit and that of the society.

Emotional Roller-coaster

Your words can't be good when they are bad, but your emotions will make you feel and think that way. As the everyday hardworking man or woman, old or young, we need a standard. Let it not be based on your emotions because it will make you change your opinions so many times, it's not funny. Therefore, you don't want to make decisions based on your emotions when it comes to matters of the heart. There are so many political and social issues now and with social media, it is easy to sway in different directions. So, the way you speak, needs to be backed up by something bigger and higher than yourself. It needs to be a positive and consistent pathway. That is why I chose the Bible as mine. You will struggle within yourself, but to have consistency and to make good progress, you need that standard.

How the Heart Responds

Your heart takes the first hit when there is a problem because that is where your treasure is. So, before you learn any step-by-step method of curbing or eliminating curse words, your heart needs to be on board. With words we speak most of the time, you may know the right thing to say, but your heart has not been invited to the party.

The formulas in this book are targeted at getting your heart right either from information that you will gain from this book or it may remind you of what you have heard, seen or read elsewhere.

Have you ever wondered why it is difficult sometimes to say, "I'm sorry," even when you are wrong? They are two powerful words that can instantly resolve years of bitterness and unforgiveness, but very difficult to utter. It's because your heart is not fully on board with the issue that needs to be dealt with accordingly. Your heart is still figuring out reasons why you shouldn't and doesn't want to dwell on the repercussions.

Andrew Peterson is a musician and his genre is Christian pop, Christian rock, folks rock, roots rock, and more. He wrote a song titled, "[I Want to Say I'm Sorry](#)" and the first two parts of the song goes like this:

I WANT TO SAY I'M SORRY

BUT I DON'T KNOW HOW –

BUT I'M SORRY.

What Is So Good About Bad Language?

I'M SO SORRY NOW. I SAID SOME WORDS TO YOU

I WISH I'D NEVER SAID.

I KNOW WORDS CAN KILL

'CAUSE SOMETHING'S DEAD

From those words, you could tell that there was a battle in the heart, to utter the words "I'm sorry."

We are very visual minded creatures and now that you can visualise what the "F" and "S" words mean when applied in a sentence, it is up to you to decide as to whether it is necessary to revert to swear words.

What comes out of your mouth, was first in your heart. To start the learning process, you therefore need to start from the heart. It is important to focus on changing yourself first and hopefully, you can influence others.

Formula

Formula 1: Love = Love Myself to Love Others

To love yourself and others may sound like a cliché but very true.

To love yourself is to acknowledge that God is your creator, first. You are fearfully and wonderfully made with value and purpose, and that is your makeup. God is Love so you have enough love in you. It is a command, a law. To love yourself is to be forgiving of yourself, allow for human error, speak kindly, be willing to serve others, and show compassion.

Seeing others as the handwork and creation of God should serve as caution over your mouth. You can speak with words that address behaviour without abusing the creation. Understanding that just as you are God's creation, so is the next person. Learning to speak well, helps us live well with others and that is how the discipline of love is built.

(Reflection: Without seeing and acknowledging the value in myself and others how can I consistently speak positively?)

Step 1: Love - Re-read Formula 1

Step 2: Love - Memorise and understand Formula 1

Step 3: Love - Tell yourself you can practise and master Formula 1

Heart Outcome

- You will automatically be ready to calm the raucous of negative words that want to surge out of your mouth.
- With an awakened heart, you will be more aware of offensive words and will become very selective of what you allow into it, either through movies, shows, or your conversations.
- Nothing good in you will encourage you to keep swearing, but something good in you will encourage you to use the right words to express yourself.

"Words have energy and power with the ability to help, to heal, to hinder, to hurt, to harm, to humiliate, and to humble." **— Yehuda Berg**

CHAPTER 2

YOU'VE GOT THE POWER

Death and life are in the power of the tongue and those who love it will eat its fruit."

– Proverbs 18:21

The Currency of Language

Then God said, "Let there be light," and there was light. – Genesis 1:3. A phrase that is echoed by the religious and non-religious alike. The power of words.

"That's one small step for a man, one giant leap for mankind." – Neil Armstrong. The power of words.

"I have a dream that my four little children will one day live in a nation where they will not be judged by the colour of their skin but by the content of their character." – Martin Luther King. The power of words.

Language is one of the most powerful gifts everyone has, even those who can't speak. A person that is dumb is not denied of this blessing. A person that is deaf is not denied of this blessing either. They may not be able to express words the way someone that can speak will do, but if their brain is active and there is consciousness, they will be able to express ideas, emotions, and signals through their actions. Those actions will be motivated by what is already in their heart.

Language is a currency and the English language is what most people use daily in communicating and transacting any business. Communicating in the language you speak is the currency that initiates the transaction before money. The same goes for any other language.

As mentioned earlier, several researches are supporting the notion that honesty is at the heart of cussing. Should we all jump on the 'honesty wagon?' I wonder the effect that will have if you are trying to carry out a business transaction.

Picture This

Now that we can visualize a few of the swear words and some of the unmentionables, let's see what it can look like.

- I feel like "faeces."
- I have a "faeces" load of work to do.
- How the "sex" am I going to get through these "faeces"?
- He was "faeces" at me.
- She is just a "female dog."
- Who the "sex" knows?
- What the "sex"?

Now, let us consider replacing those swear words with simple but everyday words that are more appropriate:

- I feel quite (tired/stressed/vulnerable/low in energy/restless).
- I have (a lot/a reasonable amount/plenty) of work to do.
- How am I going to get through this (challenge/mess/pain/exam/assignment/project/traffic)?
- He was (upset/angry/screaming/yelling) at me.
- She wasn't herself today/Her words were hurtful.
- Who really knows/That was confusing?

- What just happened? What went wrong? Can you clarify what you just said please?

A renewed mind of how to see the situation or value the other person can totally change your sentence before you even say it. It becomes obvious that it is not necessary to use abrasive or crass words. Your language can change altogether.

I Have a Question

So, is it true that unless you swear, honesty has now eluded you?

I think in most cases when swearing is a habit, it's more an indication of moral disregard in the society.

When you speak without a filter doesn't necessarily mean you are being honest. It borders a lot more on a lack of consideration to others, especially when children are around. It reflects an inadequacy of better coping skills when frustration strikes. It also shows a desire to gratify self when you use vulgar words to explain yourself.

I will encourage you not to be discouraged if cussing is not your "go-to" because it takes strength to choose to speak with respect to others. Obviously, not everyone can or will be willing to do it.

Your Words Hurt You First

Whatever you are about to say, has already being seasoned and simmered in your heart like a soup in a pot before it comes out of your mouth. You must have heard the phrase 'think before you speak' because your heart is like a ground and it will absorb whatever you put in it. Garbage in - Garbage out. So, you control what you allow to settle in your heart.

When you swear at people in anger and frustration, you are hurting yourself. The pain you want to inflict on others has already affected you first because it came out of you. That is why you feel drained and mentally exhausted after trying to explain your hurt. Just like a physical activity, it can wear you down. Before you can affect others with your words, it has already had some form of impact on you.

Therefore, as you are swearing at someone with the full intention of making them understand how stupid their action was or how hurt you are, those very words reflect your wounds.

If you can't help but speak hurtful words, it's because you are hurting, but do you have to hurt others with your words because you are hurting? Or can you receive healing by first healing others with good words? There needs to be a change in your mindset and a change in your heart. Keep reading.

Power Over Swearing

When you have power over cussing, it reflects the following about you:

- Self-control.
- You are more patient than the average person, and patience is a virtue.
- You understand that cussing yourself over water that spilled, and the traffic lights that didn't change fast enough, doesn't change the situation, it only heightens your stress level.
- Your heart is set on using better words to speak to people.
- You are not afraid to show kindness.

The Test

The International English Language Testing System (IELTS) is an internationally recognised and approved English language proficiency test for people interested in studying, working or migrating to English speaking countries like Australia, New Zealand, Canada, United Kingdom and the United States of America. It tests your ability in reading, writing, listening, and speaking in less than 3 hours. You will be refused acceptance for whatever you are applying for if you don't get set marks for the tests. The tests are only valid for 2 years and are not necessarily cheap.

What Is the Password?

I have been in Australia for over 14 years as at the time of this writing. I had to take the test and show evidence of my test results when we came to Australia and when I applied for certain jobs. You may have gained a qualification within Australia as an Adult but to get certain jobs where communication in English is vital, you must take a form of English test to prove your proficiency. Who can blame them with the degradation of grammar and loss of language? Have we become lazy in speaking, reading, writing, and listening? We can blame social media, but the fundamentals of what will make a society function in a civil and respectable manner is good communication and we have the responsibility of improving ourselves.

Christianity is a way of life. The Bible encourages us to study to show ourselves approved, speak kind words, and be diligent to do good. If you feel the Christianity movement is not your thing, then adopt its lessons as a way of life, as a truth of life. It is a good way of life if you stay true to it.

The Sieving Process

There are two types of IELTS exams. The IELTS General Training and The IELTS Academics.

The IELTS General Training test focuses on how you can apply your communication skills in engaging with others within a social and workplace context. It is relevant to those wanting to go and live, work or do a form of training in an English-speaking country. It is also a standard requirement for migration to Australia, Canada, New Zealand, and the United Kingdom.

The thought of taking this test puts a decree of dread in the hearts of those that want to enter these countries legally or without a refugee status. If you do not get the standard scores, it will affect the granting of your Visa. That is part of the advantage of being proficient in the English Language.

The IELTS Academics test, on the other hand, is for people applying to get into a higher institution like the Colleges or Universities in these countries. It considers some of the features of academic language and assesses whether you are proficient enough to begin working, studying, or training. The expectation for the Academics test is much higher than the General and if you do not meet the requirements, you will not be accepted into that field.

The good thing about the IELTS tests though is that you can always try again. However, some people have tried repeatedly and because of these high standards have not succeeded. It feels like being stuck in a rut. In some cases, not because the students are not good enough or know what they are saying or writing but because the standard has been set by widely supported institutions and trusted by several countries. If you don't succeed, you try again. There are also lots of learning opportunities before the actual test. It can be a trying period for people that want to make it through.

The Testing Ground

A program called the National Assessment Program – Literacy and Numeracy (NAPLAN) managed by the Department of Education in Australia is a fantastic program in my opinion. It is an annual assessment for students in years 3, 5, 7 and 9 designed to test skills that are essential for every child to progress through school.

NAPLAN tests these essential skills in 4 areas: speaking, writing, language conventions (spelling, grammar, and punctuation) and numeracy. It's a bit like the IELTS but for primary and high school students. It started as a paper-based exam but is now been done online as well. The outcome of the tests helps teachers tailor each child's education more effectively. I think that is a good thing for each child for their future and that of the economy.

Further Testing

On the other hand, the Online Literacy and Numeracy Assessment (OLNA) is for students who have not achieved "band 8" or above in their year 9 NAPLAN tests. If students don't meet the minimum requirement of OLNA needed to get the three different components which are Reading, Writing and Numeracy, they will not receive a Western Australian Certificate of Education (WACE) at the end of year 12. They will not be considered for University Entry in year 12. However, students have the opportunity of taking the OLNA tests twice a year in years 10, 11, and 12.

These days, it's not just foreign students that are struggling to meet these minimum requirements of numeracy and literacy. Even children that started their education in Australia are having the same issues. This could be for a range of reasons. Cussing and profanity is evidence of a decline in vocabulary. Being able to string a couple of sentences together without cussing will make for a stable, positive, and productive work environment. Hence, we have the power to influence this change by using appropriate words around children from the word go.

It is never too late to turn our words around for the better.

Loss of Language

I remember my primary school days and how the teachers kept encouraging us to speak the English language at home instead of our local languages. The idea was to allow us to practice and better retain the concepts that were being taught in class so we can become more fluent and pass our tests.

I come from Ogoni in Nigeria and it is a small tribe. I have been out of the country for a while now and I can feel some sense of loss when I don't say the words correctly due to lack of use. In Nigeria, there are so many languages and dialects that to enable effective communication, people are happy to speak pidgin or broken English within the community. Pidgin English is the language used in places like the markets, on the buses, with your neighbours, with friends, and at street shops.

Pidgin English is not swearing or cussing but a common level language for everyone and Nigerians are quite proud of it.

Some basic Pidgin English and their English translations are:

How you dey? (How are you doing?)

I dey fine, thank you. (I am fine, thank you.)

No wahala. (No problem.)

Wetin dey happen? (What is going on or what is the matter?)

E bi like say rain go fall today. (It looks like it's going to rain today.)

It is good to be able to speak your language well. There is a sense of belonging and pride in speaking your language efficiently or any other learned language that you can speak to command actions.

The Writing's on the Wall

Spanish or Mandarin are top on the list in learning another language other than your own. As every language will likely have appropriate and inappropriate slangs, you don't want to start by learning inappropriate slangs.

Before the money currency for transactions, language existed as the currency and word of promise. Even now, before any transaction, some form of communication would have occurred through verbal or written language. It holds such a powerful place in our everyday life that it cannot be spoken carelessly.

To carry out any business transaction, you need to be able to communicate. The language you use is an important part of that process. If you travel to any country and cannot speak the language, you will be very restricted on the type of jobs and opportunities you can engage in.

If cussing is a challenge for you or like myself you would want to see the language used appropriately, I will encourage you to be practical with the formula's offered if you want to see a lasting change.

Clean Comedy

There is a hunger for stand-up comedians who make us laugh and keep us happy in the hour with clean jokes.

Language doesn't have to be dirty, to be funny. They can be fun to express just as they happened, and even funnier from the mouth of an expert comedian. We have more than enough words in the dictionary to express our frustration, anger, sadness, or joy and still come out like a winner.

Below are some comedians who perform clean comedy that are suitable for the entire family to enjoy.

- Dry Bar Comedy
- Michael Jr. Comedy
- John B Crust Comedy

You will enjoy their clean comedies and would want to know more about them!

Formula

Formula 2: Joy and Peace = Less Worry and Anxiety

Joy is about having a good feeling in your heart that is not dependent on your situation. Also, peace is an inner strength to be calm even in trying situations. You can experience joy and peace because you have access to language. It is within your ability to use the positive words in that language for a greater good.

(Reflection: Without appropriately utilizing the contents of my language and the stability it provides for expressions, how will I embrace the joy and peace it can give?)

Step 1: Joy and Peace - Re-read Formula 2

Step 2: Joy and Peace - Memorise and understand Formula 2

Step 3: Joy and Peace - Tell yourself you can practice and master Formula 2

Heart Outcome

- With Joy in your heart, you have a tool that you can use to process problems in a clean language in your mind. You will be less reactive, more proactive, and more mentally alert.

- With Peace in your tool kit, you have access to explore more descriptive words, using your thesaurus, dictionary, and reading books. Use your language as your first currency to show regard for others and build stronger and genuine relationships.

"Kind words are a creative force, a power that concurs in the building up of all that is good, and energy that showers blessings upon the world." — Lawrence G. Lovasik

CHAPTER 3

A CANCER OF EMOTIONAL EXPRESSION

"If we understood the power of our thoughts, we would guard them more closely. If we understood the awesome power of our words, we would prefer silence to almost anything negative. In our thoughts and words, we create our own weaknesses and our own strengths. Our limitations and joy begin in our hearts. We can always replace negative with positive."

– Betty Eadie

The Cancer

Listen carefully to the way people speak. Stress, frustration, and anger can be heard through words. Add cussing, and it becomes a cancer that, if not managed, can consume the person. There is a higher probability of swearing and verbal abuse where there is violence because that is the nature of the word that is being born.

With your words you create life. With your words you create death. In relationships, people makeup and break up with words. Whether it is sent as a text, letter or speaking face to face. That is why you must be so careful when you use words. Like I have said earlier on, we depend on each other to survive.

Words that we speak have life and target the heart otherwise they won't hurt or make us happy as they often do. If they meant nothing, we wouldn't crave for them as we would crave for water in the desert. It makes a world of difference physically, mentally, and emotionally to hear a loved one say, "I love You," just to hear, "Thank you," just to hear, "I am sorry." If words meant nothing, we would not stay up late in the night, bawling our eyes out over what has been said or not said.

Don't You Dare Tell Me What Not to Say

You see, at your place of work, you operate with instructions by being told what to do to maximise efficiency and productivity within a team environment. You don't go into work and choose to do what you like or disrespect your boss. You will get fired. You cannot have too many bosses in the same role within an office, it is catastrophic because each person will want to assert their own authority. The reason you have a boss is for leadership, structure, and management of processes. Their presence and instructions keep you accountable in your job responsibilities and if you have any challenges, you can equally approach them. So, when they tell you what to do, you do it as long as it is within the processes of the organisation. That way you keep your job.

However, there is a side of us that doesn't like to be told what to do or not to do, especially with regards to morals or behaviours. That is the attitude of most of us. You may feel belittled and insulted to be corrected about a behaviour that is not appropriate. It is a matter of the sense of control that we want to hold onto for ourselves. Sometimes, we need to listen to the truth and do what we are told, for our own good, and let go of pride, especially were morals and behaviors are involved.

In fact, the moment you tell someone to stop swearing, using profanity, or cursing, out of spite or just for the fun of it, they may triple that behaviour just to prove that they are the boss of their own lives.

This book is not about telling anyone to stop swearing, because that doesn't work unless you train your heart. Rather, it is for each person to look around, assess their emotional reactions, and see the impact that swearing, and cussing is having in their everyday life. Then you can decide to surrender your heart to what is right and appropriate for the sake of your physical, mental, and spiritual state of mind. For the sake of the next generation.

Disabling the Able

Marriages have been known to breakdown because of to lack of effective communication. Surprise, surprise. For example, Bobby may feel frustrated that he is not understood, but he swears most of the time.

We all can build our character. Character building is not only about you but the people around you. A positive character brings help and healing to others.

It becomes frustrating then, when a perfectly capable person, feels like the only way to be heard and understood is when they swear at everything.

When you see a therapist, in as much as it is a non-judgemental environment, they will need to hear specific words from you that truly explains what is happening in your mind. It is a difficult task if the therapist is expected to do some mind-reading when every emotion and situation is explained with the "F" and "S" words. It is disabling for the client and the therapist, and that behaviour doesn't help much with the process. If you have ever been to a therapist or counsellor, you may have been presented with the "Wheel of Emotions."

The Therapist and The Chart

A psychologist, Dr Robert Plutchik expressed through the Wheel of Emotions that there are eight primary emotions that serve as the base of others. I am not here to analyse emotional patterns but to help you understand the significance of this emotional wheel when it comes to expressing what is going on in the mind. It is a chart with different words that helps a client to describe their emotions.

It is a valuable tool during counselling that helps the client pinpoint the emotions experienced because of an event. Recognising the emotions helps the client understand that deep feeling which leads to a clearer mind to deal with the problem.

Instead of throwing the "F" and "S" bombs and blaming anything and everything on somebody else, the emotion wheel helps to simplify their emotion which is very liberating. Through verbalising the primary emotion as it links to other feelings and the reactions that come with that, it creates an opportunity to express one's thoughts openly and honestly. That constructive way of expressing one's feelings, immediately empowers the individual to make an informed decision that will align with their goals.

Emotional Intelligence – The "In-Thing"

Google dictionary defines Emotional Intelligence as the capacity to be aware of, control, and express one's emotions, and to handle interpersonal relationships judiciously and empathetically.

I will say to Google, "I'm hearing you."

Emotional Intelligence, also abbreviated as EQ or EI, was created by Peter Salavoy and John Mayer but made popular by Dan Goleman who defined EI as the ability to:

1. Recognise, understand, and manage our own emotions.
2. Recognise, understand, and influence the emotions of others.

In practicality, that means being aware that emotions can drive our behaviour and impact others positively or negatively and learning how to manage those emotions — both our own and others, especially when under pressure.

Again, I will say to Dan Goleman, "I hear you."

My focus is not on the big researches but for you to really search your heart and see how vulgar words change the conversation and atmosphere.

Have you been in an environment where people are talking about their working conditions? This could be at a restaurant, in a taxi, shopping centre, cooperate office, school premises, or café. When words get thrown around, it may get nasty. There is usually a lot of bitterness, and it chokes positivity. Even when ideas and solutions that can make a difference are mentioned, they may be met with sarcasm. Such discussions breed hostility and conflict if you don't manage your emotions in that environment.

EQ Categories

These experts divided EQ into 5 categories:

1. *Self-awareness*: is about recognising your emotions as it happens. Developing awareness to identify your true feelings so that you can evaluate and manage your emotions. It involves firstly, your emotional awareness which is your ability to recognise those emotions and their effect. Secondly, your self-confidence in your ability to appreciate your self-worth and capabilities.
2. *Self-regulation*: is accepting that emotions are real and there for a reason. However, you can have control over how long it lasts by using different techniques to alleviate negative emotions like anger, anxiety, or depression. Some of these techniques are to help look at the situation in a more positive light either by stepping out of that

environment, prayer, or meditation. Self-regulation involves self-control, maintaining honesty and integrity, taking responsibility for your own actions, handling change with flexibility, and being open to new ideas.

3. *Motivation:* to stay motivated and make the effort to practice and learn to think positively and display a positive attitude to achieve your set and clear goals. Catching negative thoughts as they occur and reframe them in positive terms. Motivation involves striving to improve, commitment to your goals, recognising opportunities, and being optimistic despite obstacles and setbacks.

4. *Empathy:* being skilful at understanding the feelings behind other people's emotion's so that you can better control the signals or support you send them. To show empathy is to anticipate and recognise other's needs and help them meet that need by aiding them to appreciate their own abilities. Encouraging opportunities, seeking to see their situation through their eyes, and discerning the feelings behind their wants and needs.

5. *Social Skills:* The development of good interpersonal skills is vital in life. In today's world, information and technical

knowledge are at almost everyone's fingertips. So, people skills are even more important now because it will help you better understand, empathize, and negotiate with others in a global economy. Social skills embody learning to send a clear message to influence, inspire, encourage, and work with others towards a shared goal. It involves building bonds and the ability to understand, negotiate and resolve conflicts.

When the Attack Comes

In my opinion, swearing and carrying on with profanity may work for you for a while, but only for a while. As you deal with people and situations, it will come back and attack you. Look out for the following attacks when you continue cussing:

- It will attack your mental health.
- It will attack your relationships.
- It will attack your children.
- It will attack your ability to verbalize your emotions.
- It will attack your ability to control your emotions.
- It will attack your happiness.

Just give it time, that is the nature of the beast. It is a sin before God. The time will come when we will need to give an account of the things we've said.

Nothing good in you will encourage you to keep swearing or use profanity.

Stressing In and Out

Stress is an everyday part of life. It's everywhere and affects everyone, which is not a bad thing. Our daily living, challenges even the most well-organised life to a potential stream of stressful experiences. We are exposed to changes that range from negative extremes to physical dangers, in other to get satisfaction from desires and life successes. It is indeed an essential part of life and can act as a motivation in achieving our goals. The reality is not whether your stress is a result of major events or minor daily challenges. It's how you respond that determines the impact it will have on your life, short or long term.

Instead of letting stress, which is part of everyday life, determine your *Cuss-O-Meter*, allow your mind, no matter how hard this can be, to accept that we are not living in a perfect world. It's not all about you, so continue your journey of looking for strategies that can help you cope with stress in a more positive way.

Formula

Formula 3: Patience and Kindness = Discipline and Progress

Being patient is your ability to be courageous in challenging situations and showing kindness is agreeing to be useful in service to others. You can learn to be patient and kind as you listen to others and retrain your mind to self-communicate effectively.

(Reflection: Without an intention to practice self-communication through patience and kindness for improvement, how can I genuinely do the same with others?)

Step 1: Patience and Kindness - Re-read Formula 3

Step 2: Patience and Kindness - Memorise and understand Formula 3

Step 3: Patience and Kindness - Tell yourself you can practice and master Formula 3

Heart Outcome

- Forgiveness begins to come with ease, and you are better positioned to handle and bounce back quicker from daily and long-term stressors.
- You are now better positioned to show compassion and empathy to others that are struggling with daily and long-term stressors.

"One kind word can change someone's entire day." - **Unknown**

CHAPTER 4

WHAT ABOUT THE NEXT GENERATION?

"Words are seeds that do more than blow around. They land in our hearts and not the ground. Be careful what you plant and careful what you say. You might have to eat what you planted one day."

– Unknown

Good People Speaking Badly

Here is part of an article by Carolyn L. Todd on May 27, 2017:

Gordon Ramsay may have a superb palette, but he's also earned a reputation for being the filthiest-mouthed celebrity chef around. The Brit has spent his TV career berating chefs, restaurant owners, and culinary students on his series, including *Hell's Kitchen*, *MasterChef*, and *Kitchen Nightmares*. The title of his new show is a riff on that reputation: live cooking competition *The F Word* premieres May 31 on Fox. But according to Ramsay's eldest daughter, the 50-year-old leaves his potty mouth at work.

Matilda, 15, told British paper Waitrose Weekend that her dad keeps the language PG at home, reports The Mirror. "He does not swear at home," she said. "On telly he is like a strict teacher but when I watch him, I find it funny because it is so different from how he is at home. He's just a normal dad."

There is a generation that is coming up. They are watching and learning.

You may be at the point where you swear casually but don't be surprised when young ones swear at you. Isn't it sad to see an older person pouring out cuss words for the merest things?

No Name Calling Please

Unfortunately, some parents have resorted to calling their children names that are not appropriate, for the fun of it. When you were born, there was a reason why you were not called 'Satan' or the 'devil'. Your name is a very important part of your life. Sometimes your name speaks more about your before you arrive at a place. People have gotten job interviews just by mentioning the name of someone that has been a positive influence on them or the organisation. You are recognised by your name. That is why when you apply for a job, you are asked to include some references. The employer wants to know more about you through someone you have worked with or a person that can vouch for your character.

So, words have power, and can affect the life of the generation to come. I have heard stories of adults today who are still hurting from what their fathers have said to them when they were young. Some have associated their low self-esteem, depression, and certain setbacks in life to when they were called derogatory names like:

You are a "sh*t head...

You're just being a b**ch...

She is a sh*t bag...

You stupid pr**k...

You are a d**k head...

Why, why, why?

When Did Bad Language Become So Good?

Why would you describe a whole human being as a sexual body part or a human body waste? What stage of creation was this?

Why would you call your child or the next generation names that can impact their lives negatively knowing that words are powerful?

It takes the grammatical sense out of a sentence.

There are stories of adults that recount when, as children, their Fathers (unfortunately, a lot of the name callings have come from fathers) and sometimes mothers, have spoken words like:

You are useless, irresponsible, lazy, slow, stupid….

Good for nothing, tramp, slut…

A waste of space, an idiot, retard….

Come here you knucklehead…

Children don't forget these words easily. It is very important that we watch what we say to the next generation.

Cursing and swearing at your children is like digging a hole you would eventually fall into.

Why not use words like:

What About the Next Generation?

I love you no matter what…

You may have made a mistake, but I will be here to support you…

You are stronger than you think…

Work hard, stay focused, and you will achieve your dreams…

I hope any challenge you face makes you a stronger and better person….

I will try my best to be here for you….

We owe it to the next generation to improve our language for good so that they can pass it on to their children.

Businesses Want to Live On

Every business wants to continue and remain as a legacy. There is fierce competition between Coles, Aldi, and Woolworths. They want your business now more than ever because the competition and price wars are fierce. They need you to keep their business afloat. They cannot afford to be slack in their advertising. Likewise, if you want bad language to continue in the name of honesty, then you advertise it.

Bad words are created each time we swear or cuss. If we continue in that manner, our children pick up on the fact that instead of using appropriate words to express themselves, they need to cuss. That limits their vocabulary, and it is a negative way to vent their emotions. It is important to stop and think when you feel frustrated before acting or speaking, otherwise, you will say things that you'll regret for the rest of your life because words live on.

My Children's Account - Generational Strategies

When you open an account with a bank, before they finish the transaction with you, they will ask if you have children. The next question will be "What do you think about setting up a savings account for them?" The banks are patient because they know we are creatures of habit.

I remember when we opened our bank account, we were asked the same question. That same day, we thought, that was a brilliant idea. We can kill four birds with one stone. So, we were already at the bank sorted, with a new account. Why not open accounts for our children as well instead of having to go out and do other research and come back another day? They were only children and could change their accounts any time they wanted. So, because they were underage, for our three children at the time, we decided to have them registered under my name. That was fine then. Shortly afterwards, our first son started working at [Kentucky Fried Chicken Restaurant](#) (KFC) and needed his personal account. We both went into the bank to transfer his details into his new account, a debit card got arranged for him, and voila! Seven years later, he is still with the same bank. We didn't even consider researching other options to see what deals were available. That was child number one. Child number two turned 15, and the same thing happened. Got a job at KFC, went to the bank, cut the umbilical cord, and voila! Same thing with child number three.

My boys are now in their twenties and still with [Bankwest](#). My daughter is currently in her teens and is most likely going to stick with the bank. Not that it is a bad thing, but I want you to appreciate how the whole process connected the next generation.

Not Just for Today

You see, the banks had a long-term goal. They were patient. When we were signing up, they were not just interested in us as the parents, they were interested in our children as well. They too may end up getting married and remain with the same bank and do exactly what we did, with their children.

Why have I taken the time to explain this? It is because the devil is also patient. Now the research is presenting the information that people that swear are more honest. So, let's all start swearing.

If you buy into this lie, you will begin that habit in your home, day in day out. Instead of using appropriate ways to speak to your children, you will limit your vocabulary and theirs. They will cuss instead of expressing their actual frustration. Communication becomes an issue. When they are happy, they will cuss, when they are sad, they will cuss. At the same time, you are all creating verbal pollution in the house that has been linked to causing violence and verbal abuse.

With no proper training at home on how to express their emotions healthily, they start with swearing before anything else. At that stage, it becomes what they understand because that is what they have grown up with.

An Appealing Habit?

Bad habits are very dangerous. It sounds appealing initially but then it traps you and you live in shame and regret until you can break free.

In the book of Genesis 4:6-7 God's conversation with Cain went like this: "So the Lord said to Cain, "Why are you angry? And why has your countenance fallen? If you do well, will you not be accepted? And if you do not do well, sin lies at the door. And its desire is for you, but you should rule over it."

The devil is always looking for an opportunity to strike. He carries sin and destruction in his backpack, looking for who to deceive, making it look appealing. Once you have bought into the lie, you are already on the road to destruction.

God made Cain aware that sin is just outside his door. Sin wants you. It wants to control you. Please don't let it in. Take it easy. That is the same trick that is being used today. Sin is lurking around.

Trust me, you do not want to see or hear your children talking back at you or swearing and calling you names. It will hurt.

Some children have not grown up with swearing in their homes but have been influenced by peers. That is where the strategies in this book will come in handy. Bring understanding to their hearts for a lasting change.

We Live For Each Other

It is always important to remember that we don't live for ourselves. We are incomplete when we live only to satisfy ourselves. Today's generation may be promoting the "I" mentality, but it doesn't work long term. It creates conflict in relationships because later in life, it becomes difficult to reconcile why 'it's no longer all about me.'

It is not impossible to recover but why go through a painful rehab and recovery path when you can use the truth today and set yourself and a whole generation free.

Choosing not to swear as an individual and as a parent is not just about you. You are thinking of preserving the authenticity of a language. You are promoting positive relationships. You are displaying strength and self-control. You are contributing to world peace. I could go on and on. What you do today, is not just about you. Every business intends to expand and make a profit. Most couples want to have children in their marriage when possible because of the joy and the blessing they bring. Therefore, it is important to model good behaviour to them. When thinking about contributing to society, your words are one of the most subtle yet productive ways of contributing to a better society.

The Good Success

It's not every success that is a good success. It is not every success that gives peace. Don't envy people that are not doing the right thing but seem like they are enjoying life. You don't know what they are going through. The Bible has a lot to say about this kind of success.

The success you should be interested in is a success that is gained from working with integrity, trusting in God in your daily business decisions, working and giving back to the community through your Church or volunteering in other community clubs. It is living a life of prayer, fasting, and growing your relationship with Christ to gain peace. His way gives peace even when there is storm everywhere. He knows your weakness anyway. I have heard testimonies of people saying as soon as they gave their lives to Christ, all that swearing instantly ceased and they felt clean.

Monkey See Monkey Do

When you talk the talk, do you walk the walk? This generation is watching. The "do as I say but not as I do" will not last for long with any generation. They will catch on and do as you do and even better or worse. Children indeed learn better without conflicting ideas when your words support your actions.

Children will imitate because they are watching. Have you seen children trying to vacuum like mummy or wash the car like daddy? Your child will want to do the dishes as well and that will probably slow you down for the rest of the day because you want to keep them safe. Let them grow up and you won't see them anywhere near those dishes!

A lot of things we do today, is not just for ourselves. You bring discipline into your life because of the next generation. Most ladies who smoked or drank before pregnancy will usually do 180 degrees turnaround from that habit as soon as they are pregnant. That is an action from the heart for the sake of the precious child.

How amazing is that! For some, it becomes a permanent change, but others still go back to that habit after delivery. But in that brief window, there is so much power. For the love of the next generation. For the love of your child.

Potty Mouth Needs a Lot of Soap

Having three or four children in the house that all swear at the drop of a hat will be a very dramatic and emotionally charged house. If it is a habit that has not taken over the home, you will have the confidence to teach them better behaviour as it is not a standard in your home. Nip it in the bud. But if you cuss as well, you don't have any legs to stand on. Get ready with lots of soap to wash their mouths but also prepare yourself for an attitude that may want to resist change. Start retraining your heart.

The Religious Move

There are still lots of parents interested in taking their children to Christian Private schools, even those that don't want to have anything to do with God. Isn't that interesting? It is much more than the programs available. There is still a level of serenity and focus on moral preservation that exceeds that of public schools. Who doesn't want what is best for their child? In most of these religious schools, swearing is not taken lightly because of the standards of the schools. I think that is a good thing.

Note that, I am not promoting private schools, but if you can afford it, good for you. If parents swear at home, the children will pick that up and swear at school. My Children attended public schools and don't have any reason to swear at school because we don't do so at home. A parent's influence cannot be underestimated when it comes to building good or bad character.

Formula

Formula 4: Goodness = Transformed Character

Goodness in your character is action based on a desire to please God in what you do and not to please people.

(Reflection: Without acting in a way that pleases God how can I enjoy the goodness that exists?)

Step 1: Goodness - Re-read Formula 4

Step 2: Goodness - Memorise and understand Formula 4

Step 3: Goodness - Tell yourself you can practise and master Formula 4

Heart Outcome

- You will recognise that your language affects the next generation. There is a renewed determination to protect the next generation through the language you speak.
- Your heart is now equipped to see more goodness and it will reflect as true happiness from inside and out. Your words will be less abrasive.
- You will begin to experience calmness and better control of your emotions around other people.

"Be mindful when it comes to your words. A string of some that don't mean much to you may stick with someone else for a lifetime." – Rachel Wolchin

CHAPTER 5

THE RISE OF CUSSING – THE GLOBAL WARMING EFFECT

"Handle them carefully, for words have more power than atom bombs."

– Pearl Strachan Hurd

The Workplace

One of my roles as an Emergency Medical Dispatcher (EMD) is to receive ambulance emergency (000) and non-emergency calls made within Western Australia. I deliver lifesaving instructions, including first aid advise while communicating compassion to callers before the Ambulance arrives. With the nature of my job, I receive calls from the community, and it could be from someone experiencing high levels of emotional stress. The call could also come from concerned family members, friends, colleagues, or bystanders that have witnessed a situation that needs immediate medical attention.

Receiving those calls can be stressful as an EMD when callers turn their emotional stress on you with words like:

- "Get the ambulance right now you stupid c**t".
- "You're full of sh*t, just get the ambulance here now".
- Someone is going die now, you f**k head if you keep asking silly questions".

Do these sentences make grammatical, generational, environmental, and emotional sense? However, that is a stress response for some people who would otherwise not dream of speaking in an abusive manner to anyone. That been said, there are better ways and appropriate languages to use when stressed, rather than spreading that emotional cancer on others.

Again, unless understanding and change comes from the heart, it will remain an issue.

If you *normally* engage in swearing when you are happy or emotionally stressed, this could be you:

- talking to someone else in a degrading manner.

- affecting the next generation negatively without meaning to.
- polluting the environment through your words

If you apply the formulas in this book or *do not normally* engage in swearing when you are happy or emotionally stressed, this will *NOT* be you:

- talking to someone else in a degrading manner.
- affecting the next generation negatively without meaning to.
- polluting the environment through your words.

Our Footprint

Our footprint becomes a pathway others close to us will walk. When we change direction, they too will change direction. When those behind us hear of a better way, they may choose to investigate, and that additional information will empower them to make that change despite the closeness we have.

Change starts with the decision that comes from the heart, then spoken, written, or acted on. But it all comes from the heart.

At the beginning of this book, I gave a clear visual of the meaning of what we are saying when we continually cuss. It's like throwing faeces everywhere.

Instant Pollution

There is instant pollution when you swear at yourself, other people, or things. Yes, everybody gets frustrated, angry, sad, happy, disgusted, but cussing at the situation is like playing dodgeball. The ball is still the ball, but it gets thrown around all through the game. Nothing has changed except the fact that you just released some more pollution into the atmosphere. You can solve the problem without polluting the environment.

There is stress and frustration everywhere and every day, but it depends on how you see and deal with it. Your parcel didn't come in the mail and the seller had promised it will be delivered today. Dinner was not appealing and worst still, was too salty. You received a text message from the school that your child was absent, please explain. You have a trolley full of food and at the checkout, you find that your wallet is not in your bag. How embarrassing. So, where do you start and stop with the swearing?

Try counting how many times people around you throw the "S" word around in a day. Visualize the mess it creates and now try to clean it!! Or better still, look for who will clean up the mess!!

Get into day two and have the same visuals on and note how you feel emotionally, mentality, and physically afterwards.

My point is words have life. When we speak, things are created. It is no different when we are swearing. We are releasing mess into the atmosphere. Even if a few people make the mess, everyone will no doubt suffer the consequences one way or another.

The Cow and Human Effect

Dictionary.com defines Global Warming as an increase in the earth's average atmospheric temperature that causes corresponding changes in climate, and that may result from the greenhouse effect.

Everywhere you turn today, you will hear about Global Warming. The young are anxious about their future and organising climate change rallies across nations. This is not a global warming summit but for the everyday people, you hear terminologies like greenhouse emissions. Methane release in the atmosphere from cows and sheep, and rice production is thrown in the mix. Landfills, gas and oil rigs, and many other greenhouse gas emission sources are now a bigger concern. I will add swearing to the mix. Swearing is a source of greenhouse emission as well!

We have a generation of people coming up that we hope will continue to take on the challenge of climate change in ways that will directly help deal with the problem. The more people that are ready to contribute to society without the use of abrasive words the better for the leaders and others to listen and act.

You may think about your language and ask yourself "does it really matter?" But also listen and reflect on what you hear around you and through different forms of media and ask yourself again, "Is it changing for the better or can I make a positive difference with my language?"

The Most Sustainable Way to Live

As at the time of writing this book, our daughter Funmi, was attending Lynwood Senior High School, Parkwood, in Western Australia. It is an independent public co-educational specialist school that prides itself in sustainability. We were not within the school's catchment but applied for the specialist program called Environment and Life Sciences (EaLs). She is presently in year 11 and has graduated from the program which runs from year 7 to 10. This is not a science class, but I can tell you, our house is not the same again as the result of the influence and information she brought home for a more sustainable way to live. You name it, she rebuked us, and we learnt a lot from her.

She engaged in conversations about recycling, water management, switching off lights, and good products to use. It was encouraging to see the confidence in practising what she has been taught at school that was making an impact in its own way. Besides those environmental benefits, her confidence and social skills also improved. What a bonus.

I listen better about recycling, not because of the media only, but also because my daughter keeps telling me about it! I considered it a good thing and I am very proud that I can listen to her, mostly about sustainability!

It comes down to me being an example for her to see because what she said made sense for us and the environment. Likewise, because of my understanding of the impact of cussing mentally, physically, socially, and spiritually, we also stand to be an example for her to see. That is love, and what makes the world go round.

Formula

Formula 5: Faithfulness = Consistence in Truth

To be faithful is a decision to be steadfast in the truth you have discovered. It is important to constantly improve your language to better express yourself.

(Reflection: Without aiming towards improving my language, how can I be a blessing to my environment?)

Step 1: Faithfulness - Re-read Formula 5

Step 2: Faithfulness - Memorise and understand Formula 5

Step 3: Faithfulness - Tell yourself you can practise and master Formula 5

Heart Outcome

- Your heart is now prepared to make your change long term as a contribution to environmental clean-up and a practical sustainable living experience.
- You will begin to see yourself more and more as part of the solution to a better society.

"No matter what anybody tells you, words and ideas can change the world." — John Keating

CHAPTER 6

WHEN YOU CAN'T HELP YOURSELF

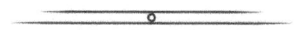

"Don't mix bad words with your bad mood. You'll have many opportunities to change a mood, but you'll never get the opportunity to replace the words you spoke."

— Unknown

God-Given Self Control

Cussing might start as a joke, here and there. How long does someone need to hear the same joke before it loses its flavour? When will the traffic stop making you swear? What about the string of bad news on television? What about the good game you played? When is the right time and age to make the change?

Whatever happens in your life will affect your heart one way or another. Difficulties and experiences are all different, but the emotions will target the heart. It doesn't matter how educated, skilled, talented, rich, or poor, you are, the bus stop for the challenges in life is the heart.

News Flash – "The Name Jesus"

Do you know that the name "Jesus" is not a swear word?

Have you heard about the Christmas story or the reason why Christmas is celebrated around the world? It is because of Jesus. The story of Christmas is the commemoration of the birth of Jesus Christ as God on earth to confirm the assurance that as human beings, we have a purpose on earth. Your life here is not the end, no matter how good or bad it has been. There is something bigger and greater. He lived a life without sin and rejected no one but He warned everyone to live a life that honours God.

He lived on earth, healed the sick, raised the dead, died, and rose, and was witnessed and recorded as the truth by many. After His resurrection into heaven, His disciples continued His work and also performed many miracles in His name. The name of Jesus. He declared Himself as the son of God. He was revealed in the Bible within the Old Testament and His existence became a reality in the New Testament. He is the God and creator of human beings as we know it and He is very merciful, regardless of what we have done and how many have rejected and walked away from Him.

My dear friends, the name 'Jesus' is not a swear word. It is a very powerful name in prayer for Christians and anyone who chooses not to live for themselves but to live for Jesus Christ. At the name of Jesus, with understanding and reverence, demons flee, and lives are transformed.

The Easter Story

Have you heard of Good Friday and the Easter Celebration? It is because of the death and resurrection of Jesus Christ.

The Easter is an evidence of the Christian faith. Without the story of the death and resurrection of Jesus Christ there is no Christianity. But He came on earth to confirm the Old Testament and to tell us about the Kingdom of God that is coming. The purpose of His death was to bear the sins of the whole world and by His resurrection, anyone that asks for His forgiveness is redeemed and can make a fresh start. He left commandments and instructions that are the foundations, ethics, and values of nations after nations. A lot of community organisations, businesses, and not-for-profit companies were founded based on the principles of the Word of God.

But today, a lot of what we know as the Bible and Word of God has been lost in transition and translation. Individuals have become their own gods, rely on their own understanding, and define their own moral standards. Needs and wants are pursued to satisfy the 'self'. The spiritual disconnection from our God, which psychologists today have come to realise that it's a fundamental part of us as humans, have left many handicap. Some don't know where to start from to find that spiritual connection.

Today I plead with you that, to repeatedly use the name of Jesus Christ in vain and in combination with other swear words is not a good thing.

Jesus Christ is the reason why we have Christianity today. The Bible is His word and the moral compass that sustains many people. He gave commandments, which are laws for us to live by on earth till He returns to judge the world of the good and evil. His word purifies and sanctifies the human heart to bring the change we need. Every command He gave is not to frustrate but to help us live a better life with each other until we leave the earth, or He returns, whichever comes first.

I understand that no one likes to be told what to do because that is how the flesh operates. A desire to be the king of our world, to say and do what we like. That is not what Jesus has called us to do because He knows the consequences that we bring on ourselves and others with such a mindset.

You may not like what I am about to say, but unless you stop using the name of Jesus Christ, the God of gods, and the Lord of lords in vain, at the end of your life on earth, you will be held accountable.

The 3rd Commandment

The 3rd commandment in the Bible says, "You shall not take the name of the Lord your God in vain". It is a commandment for a reason.

Have you seen people that live in mansions and seem like they have it all together from the outside but on the inside don't have inner peace? Jesus promises a peace that all your possessions in this world cannot give to you. He promises a life of peace here on earth and beyond when you call on His name, not as a swear word but as your Lord and Saviour, and when you recognise Him as a part of your life. He doesn't force anyone to come to Him but waits patiently for an invitation.

If you believe in God, it is a sin to take the name of Jesus Christ in vain. Just like you must take responsibilities for your actions and bear the consequences in your everyday life, likewise there are consequences for disobeying the Word of God that will affect you spiritually and manifest physically. But more than that, the consequences of disobeying the Word of God, especially taking His name in vain, will follow us in death, unless we repent and confess our sins. Continue reading to know how you can do this and be free.

The 5th Commandment

The 5th Commandment in the Bible is 'Honour your father and your mother'.

How would you feel if someone were to speak rudely to your parents and intentionally try to hurt them? It hits your very core and it is a dishonour to you. Your blood connection can fill you with so much rage that you may accidentally commit a serious crime. That is how strong that connection is because, blood is thicker than water as they say. But Jesus says, turn the other cheek and apply wisdom to address such situations. Why? Our anger may cause us to sin, which does not reflect the righteousness of God in us. As difficult as that is to accept, it is the truth. He says, vengeance belongs to Him. We need to keep applying wisdom when faced with situations that affect our very core.

Swearing with the name of "Jesus" is a sin.

Please do not abuse and swear at your parents no matter what they have done to you. Rather, pray for them, and ask Jesus to give you a heart of forgiveness toward them, and He will answer your prayers.

The Heart Speaks

Our hearts are open and therefore vulnerable. As such, the way we respond to things reflects the state of our heart. In a situation, one person might be calm, indifferent, or reflective and another person may be angry, frustrated, or aggressive.

In situations like this, when the "F" and the "S" words start shooting out, it is simply the reflection of the heart.

When a relationship has ended, one person might say, "My heart is broken;" "She broke my heart." Even though a broken heart might heal, it has been touched by that experience. Such experiences change the demeanour of the person for a while. That means you must be careful of what you allow in and out of your heart because of the resultant effect it may have on you and others.

Sucked Prayers

Can you imagine something being sucked into a vortex? That is what happens when you are a repeat offender of cussing and swearing. Your growth is being sucked into a vortex; your relationship is being dragged into a vortex, your prayer is being sucked into a vortex until you are ready to start cleaning up your heart to allow for true growth.

You must understand that when your words have been stolen through swearing, you bring a strain on yourself and create a distance between you and God.

Give your heart to God because out of the abundance of the heart the mouth speaks. Before any word comes out of your mouth, it has gone through your heart. If you are challenged by the desire to always swear when there is traffic, the door slams, or you are late for an appointment, then the devil will be very happy with you. That is not what you want. We communicate with God through the words of our mouth. Why would you use the same mouth that you praise God with to curse yourself and other people? James 3:10 says, "Out of the same mouth proceed blessing and cursing. My brethren, these things ought not to be so."

God Is Interested in Your Words

God is interested in what comes out of your mouth.

He created the world with declarations and there is so much power when we declare words as well.

Imagine one moment, speaking the "F" "S" and "B" words or taking the name of God in vain and the next moment, going down on your knees to pray. The devil will be very happy with this. It's like you have created so much mess around you each time before coming to God in praise and prayer. Your first task then is to start by cleaning up the filth that has just come out of your mouth through asking for forgiveness. God is ever forgiving and merciful, then you can start praying because he is a Holy God. Don't let anyone deceive you.

Exodus 20:7 says, "You shall not take the name of the Lord your God in vain, for the Lord will not hold him guiltless who takes His name in vain."

Consistent in Growth

God wants to see us grow in our relationship with Him, not starting from the beginning each time. We delay our destiny by being disobedient. God doesn't hate us. He wants us to wake up from our childish behaviour and be so hungry for him that the things of this world will grow dim in our eyes.

There is a scripture that a lot of people might not be aware of that says:

"If anyone among you thinks he is religious and does not bridle his tongue but deceives his own heart, this one's religion is useless."

– James 1:26

When you can't help yourself, Jesus is there for you, always.

Repent Daily

A permanent cure for swearing, cussing or profanity is to confess your weakness to God and truly ask him to tame your tongue. Let your fear for God be greater than your desire to join in a conversation or be funny in front of your friends.

To genuinely repent daily before God, say a simple prayer like: *"Lord Jesus, I want to use my mouth to praise you. Please forgive me of all my sins and of the times I have taken your name in vain. Take over my emotions, let me use them in a way that pleases you. I don't want to get angry and swear at everything because I know that doesn't help my relationship with you. I know you love me. Let me be more aware of You in my life. I surrender my life to you and thank you because you hear me always in Jesus name. Amen."*

Formula

Formula 6: Gentleness = Repentant Heart

Being gentle is developing calmness and a heart of humility that is ready to repent and change bad behaviour in yourself and be forgiving toward others.

(Reflection: Without compassion how can I be forgiving?)

Step 1: Gentleness - Re-read Formula 6

Step 2: Gentleness - Memorise and understand Formula 6

Step 3: Gentleness - Tell yourself you can practice and master Formula 6

Heart Outcome

- You understand that forgiveness is within reach daily and you will no longer be easily frustrated but better prepared to know what you allow into your heart.
- You will be more aware that in good and bad times, you can still trust God and He is merciful and willing to guide you to a better you daily.

"Don't ever diminish the power of words. Words move hearts and hearts move limbs." – Hamza Yusuf

CHAPTER 7

THE BEAUTIFUL TRUTH

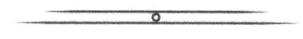

"Kind words can be short and easy to speak, but their echoes are truly endless."

– Mother Teresa

Surrender, Obedience and Blessings

You receive wages from an organisation for the services you provide but you work for God. It is God that gives you life and longevity and sustains you daily. It is through living by His standards and principles that you get a better life. That is why every day, it is necessary to pray and ask for more of Him and less of you.

It doesn't matter how smart, rich, good, strong, and confident you are, it doesn't matter the kind of strategies you are putting in place daily to live a life of peace; it doesn't matter how many trainings and seminars you attend; these are great things and necessary in life.

But there is one thing that tops it all, that crowns it all. It is the truth that we all need good and positive help. A help that is bigger and better than each of us. That help is from Jesus that loves us so much. To fill that vacuum. To complete that sense of purpose.

At the end of the day, we all need hope that we have a good reason to live another day. We need to see the good in situations and people when bad things have happened so that we can gradually gain strength from that vision. We need an understanding of the grace, mercy, and truth of God as the creator so that we can have peace that even when we struggle and don't understand, He's got our back.

Leave the Controlling to God

At home, when I feel overwhelmed, frustrated, and angry, my lifeline is to call out to God. I call out to God in surrender. When I feel that my heart is being affected in a situation, I call out to God in surrender.

It is very easy to get too busy in the day and miss out on protecting your heart from the daily challenges. It is so easy to get carried away, feeling that you are in control of a situation, when in fact, you are not. It is very important to guard your heart daily. Proverbs 4:23 says: "Keep your heart with all diligence, for out of it springs the issues of life."

Learn to Praise

I have learnt that when you let those words of praise and appreciation of God come from your lips something happens in your heart. The situation might not change, but as he has promised in Philippians 4:6-7, "Be anxious about nothing but in everything by prayer and supplication with thanksgiving, let your request be made known to God and the peace that surpasses all understanding will guide your heart and mind through Christ Jesus."

What we all need is peace. Challenges will come. Unexpected situations will come and there is absolutely nothing we can do about it. But if we trust that God sees and knows all things and that He is in control, then we will gain peace.

God is not surprised by the way we speak; he is not surprised by the things we do, but he is very patient and ever inviting us to come closer to Him.

God is interested in the fact that we are trying to be better, not that we are perfect because he already has a plan for our shortcomings. He gave His son Jesus Christ to die on the cross for us. He is always interceding on our behalf.

He doesn't force his will on us. He has given us the power to choose.

Don't' Be A Walking Corpse.

"But he who sins against Me wrongs his own soul; All those who hate Me love death." **– Proverbs 8:36**

God says if we have Him, we have life. Trust God. Life is too hard and too many things are out of your control for you to try and take on the world or do it on your own.

Be grateful for life. Don't worship the creation, worship the Creator.

Pray for forgiveness and ask God to take over your life and help you in this journey called life.

True Meditation

Meditate on the word of God, not on your problems. Meditate on His love, kindness, protection, and provision by talking about His mercy and goodness.

Join a Church and don't go there looking for perfect people because we are all broken. It is a ground where you can begin to practise being closer to God. Don't be surprised if you don't feel loved in the Church, it's only a feeling at that moment. But be prepared to give love because everyone there is also looking for genuine love.

Your healing is a process, in your quiet time, invite God to speak to you through the Bible, His word.

He knows you as you are. His grace and mercy are so good that people struggle with understanding how it is possible that despite what they have done, they can be accepted and forgiven as they are. That is a miracle, just accept it by faith.

Don't be discouraged, start your journey, and ask God into your life today.

A song titled "Known" by Tauren Wells explains the love of God for us in the simplest terms. Check it out on YouTube.

Formula

Formula 7: Self-Control = Balanced Emotions and Desires

Having self-control is about admitting what areas in your life need change and be willing to put the effort in to see the change come through. If you struggle to see, hear, and speak with a positive mindset, it will be easier if you surrender yourself to God and invite him on this journey with you.

(Reflection: Without being an example with my words, how can I teach others?)

Step 1: Self-Control: Re-read Formula 7

Step 2: Self-Control: Memorise and understand Formula 7

Step 3: Self-Control: Tell yourself you can practise and master Formula 7

Heart Outcome

- You can truly eliminate cussing by surrendering your heart and your words to Jesus daily.
- Your heart has accepted that you are God's creation. You are special and gifted to be a blessing to others to the glory of God.

So, When Did Bad Language Become So Good?

You tell me.

Reference List

Bernock, D. (2018). *What Does it Mean to Love Your Neighbor as Yourself?* [online] Crosswalk.com. Available at: https://www.crosswalk.com/faith/spiritual-life/what-does-it-mean-to-love-your-neighbor-as-yourself.html [Accessed 21 Nov. 2019].

Davis, M., Elizabeth Robbins Eshelman and Mckay, M. (2008). *The relaxation & stress reduction workbook.* sixth edition ed. Oakland, Ca: New Harbinger Publications.

Dorothy Kelley Patterson, Kelley, R. and Jan Lynette Dargatz (2006). *The woman's study Bible : the New King James Version.* Nashville: T. Nelson.

@faithlife. (2019). *THE FRUIT OF THE SPIRIT: Patience and Kindness.* [online] Available at: https://sermons.faithlife.com/sermons/442593-the-fruit-of-the-spirit:-patience-and-kindness [Accessed 21 Nov. 2019].

GotQuestions.org (2012). *The Fruit of the Holy Spirit – What is faithfulness? | GotQuestions.org.* [online] GotQuestions.org. Available at: https://www.gotquestions.org/fruit-Holy-Spirit-faithfulness.html [Accessed 21 Nov. 2019].

Reference List

https://www.facebook.com/JohnPiper (2015). *What's the Difference Between Peace and Joy?* [online] Desiring God. Available at: https://www.desiringgod.org/interviews/whats-the-difference-between-peace-and-joy [Accessed 21 Nov. 2019].

Ielts.org. (2019). *IELTS Introduction Learn all about the IELTS test.* [online] Available at: https://www.ielts.org/what-is-ielts/ielts-introduction.

Naijalingo.com. (2019). *no wahala.* [online] Available at: http://www.naijalingo.com/words/no-wahala [Accessed 21 Nov. 2019].

O'connor, J.V. (2006). *Cuss control : the complete book on how to curb your cursing.* Lincoln, Nebraska: Iuniverse.

Picard, C. (2017). *If You Swear a Lot, You're More Honest — Science Says So.* [online] Good Housekeeping. Available at: https://www.goodhousekeeping.com/life/news/a42172/swearing-honesty-study/ [Accessed 21 Nov. 2019].

PositivePsychology.com. (2017). *The Emotion Wheel: What It Is and How to Use It [+PDF].* [online] Available at: https://positivepsychology.com/emotion-wheel/ [Accessed 21 Nov. 2019].

Psych Central. (2018). *What is Emotional Intelligence (EQ)?* [online] Available at: https://psychcentral.com/lib/what-is-emotional-intelligence-eq/.

Wa.edu.au. (2017). *NAPLAN - Department of Education.* [online] Available at: https://www.education.wa.edu.au/naplan.

Milton Keynes UK
Ingram Content Group UK Ltd.
UKHW012253270324
440206UK00005B/380